CW00515714

Signed
by the
author

with best wishes
from.

Tom Slack

T.S.

Mousehole. Cornwall. 91

INTERESTING THINGS ABOUT BIRDS

Also by Tom Slack:

Happy is the Day — A Spitfire Pilot's Story
Thody Bros. — Unusual Window Cleaners

INTERESTING THINGS ABOUT BIRDS

Tom Slack

UNITED WRITERS
Cornwall

UNITED WRITERS PUBLICATIONS LTD
Ailsa, Castle Gate, Penzance, Cornwall.

All Rights Reserved. No part of this publication may be reproduced, stored in a retrieval system, or transmitted, in any form or by any means, electronic, mechanical, photocopying, recording or otherwise, without the prior permission of the Copyright owner.

British Cataloguing in Publication Data
Slack, Tom
Interesting things about birds.
1. Birds
I. Title
598

ISBN 1 85200 023 6

Copyright (c) Tom Slack 1989

Printed in Great Britain by
United Writers Publications Ltd
Cornwall

To the dedicated Staff and Volunteers
at the Mousehole Wild Bird Hospital,
which will receive a share of the
royalties from this book.

CONTENTS

INTRODUCTION

There are now so many field guides and books about birds and bird-watching that I have tried to make this one different by just concentrating on some interesting things about common birds.

As this is not a text book, the birds in each chapter have been arranged in alphabetical order, for easy reference, rather than placing them in the customary systematic order proposed by Wetmore of the USA and revised by Voous of Holland, which starts with the most primitive species, like the Divers and Grebes, and ends with the most highly developed perching birds, or passerines, like the Buntings and Sparrows. The only exception is the placing of the Fulmar at the end for reasons which will become apparent.

Ornithologists have strict rules about when it is correct or wrong to use a capital letter when referring to a bird or a species, but these rules have not always been followed in this book because the subtleties might be lost on the average reader, but anyone taking up bird-watching seriously should be aware that such rules exist.

I hope this little book will encourage people to take up this most enjoyable of hobbies because it is free and lasts a lifetime.

I am most grateful to David Oats for reading the original

manuscript to check for inaccuracies — David is an ornithologist living near Hayle Estuary in Cornwall, and few people know more about birds than he does. I am also grateful to Christine Fremantle for checking and improving my English and punctuation.

Tom Slack — Mousehole, Cornwall. 1989

1

ANATOMY

To enjoy bird-watching and understand bird behaviour it helps to have a basic knowledge of how a bird's body has evolved since prehistoric times when we all shared reptiles as our common ancestors.

In a bird's case, the forelimbs have developed into wings but the bone structure is not too dissimilar from our own arms, with an elbow, a wrist and a hand with rudimentary traces of a thumb and third finger. Scales have developed into feathers, except on a bird's foot as can be seen by anyone buying a broiler chicken or Christmas turkey. The feathers attached to the thumb form what is called a bastard-wing, or alula, which can be used to reduce stalling speed, like slots are used on the leading edges of aircraft wings for the same reason. The tail feathers are used to help steer the bird and act as a break on landing, like an aircraft's rudder, ailerons and flaps. A bird's hind-limbs or legs are also not dissimilar from our own, but the knee is usually hidden by feathers and what looks like the knee is really

11

the ankle, otherwise it would be bending the wrong way, and what looks like the lower leg is really the foot so that most birds, like ballerinas and fleet-footed mammals, have learnt to walk and run on their toes.

When primitive birds like Divers and Grebes come on land they shuffle along awkwardly on their feet and not on their toes, and this also occurs with some oceanic birds like Petrels, Shearwaters and Fulmars which only come on land to breed.

The number of vertebrae in a bird's neck vary considerably, depending on the need for flexibility, from 25 in a Swan to 16 in a Sparrow and 13 in some Cuckoos and Song birds down to 3 in some Pigeons, compared with 7 in all humans and most mammals, including, believe it or not, the long-necked Giraffe.

Birds prefer to face into the wind when resting or perching, and they will always take off or land into the wind if possible, whether on water or on the ground. The passerine birds which perch on branches or similar objects can avoid the possibility of falling off while roosting and sleeping, or in high winds, by crouching and bending their legs which locks their grip around the perch, and they must straighten up again to release this grip before they can move or fly away.

Birds feet have evolved to suit their habitat and way of life, with three toes forward and one backwards for perching birds, webbed feet or lobed toes for the swimmers, although the Moorhen has neither, and four webbed toes forward for Cormorants, Shags and Gannets for accelerating under water after fleeing fish, and four toes forward for Swifts to cling to and climb up vertical surfaces, and two toes forward and two backwards on Woodpeckers to help them climb up the bark of trees, and so on.

Most surface swimming birds have developed broad bodies to keep them afloat, but the bodies of Coots and Moorhens are narrow, like those of Bitterns and Rails, to enable them to move more freely through thick reed-beds. Although the Moorhen spends much of its time on water, it does not even have lobed toes, like Coots and Grebes, but long thin toes like the Jacanas or Lily-trotters of the tropics which enable them to walk on floating vegetation.

Similarly birds' beaks or bills have evolved to suit their feeding habits. The seed-eaters have short tough beaks, and the insectivorous birds have slender bills. Birds of prey have hooked beaks and the Waders have pointed bills of different shapes and sizes so that they will not compete directly with others for food, and some beaks are designed for filtering and others for skimming. A typical example of adaptation is the short bill and gaping mouth of the Swift to catch insects on the wing, compared with its close relative, the Humming-bird, which has a long bill and tubular tongue to suck nectar from blossoms.

The words beak and bill are synonymous, as far as birds are concerned, but I tend to think of beaks as stout or strong and a bill as slender, accepting that the Crossbill seems to contradict this theory although the Grosbeak gives it support.

2

BLACKBIRDS AND THRUSHES

Over the years different birds have been thought to be the most numerous in the British Isles. There have been the Sparrows, although a detailed census of Sparrows presents difficulties, and the Starling, but half our Starling population are only winter visitors from Northern Europe and Russia. The Hedge Sparrow, or Dunnock, was at one time given this honour until farming practices changed and hedgerows began to disappear, and then it was the Chaffinch until the extensive use of poisonous insecticides and herbicides on farmland caused its decline, and for a time it was thought to be the Wren until it suffered from a series of severe winters.

Although these last three have recovered in number it is now the Blackbird which wears the numerical crown, and it is believed there could be as many as fifteen to twenty million throughout the British Isles. Apart from its apparent hardiness, the Blackbird's habitat and diet is more varied than the average bird which could be factors in its obvious success.

The Blackbird's song is beautiful, and some people consider

it almost equal to that of the Nightingale. The Blackbird, with the Robin, is the last bird to sing at night and the first to greet the dawn, and, where there are street lights in a town or village, it can often be heard singing far into the night, giving local residents the impression that they have a Nightingale in the district. It is also the watch-dog of the bird world, giving its strident alarm calls as an early warning of threatening danger.

The male Blackbird is black and very territorial in the breeding season, when its beak turns a bright yellowy-orange and a ring of similar colour surrounds its eyes. The female is dark brown with faint spots on the breast, and the brownish young have fairly pronounced speckled breasts like the young of other members of the Thrush family.

The song of the Song Thrush is possibly even sweeter than the Blackbird's, but it is shorter and repetitive, which tends to reduce the effect. The Song Thrush has not fared so well as the Blackbird because it is frailer and less catholic in its choice of food, and fewer seem to be seen these days in gardens.

The larger and greyer Mistle Thrush has an undulating flight, which is more like a Woodpecker than other Thrushes, and its stance is more erect than that of the Song Thrush. Also, during gales and stormy weather it can often be heard belting out its song from the top of a tree into the wind, either in defiance or for pure joy, which is how it earned its old name of Storm Cock.

It is to be hoped that these old names will never disappear completely, because they are so much more descriptive and interesting than some of the modern ones, like Windhover for the Kestrel, Merehen for the Moorhen, and Nettlecreeper for the Whitethroat. Now some Common Market Bureaucrat has even come up with the ridiculous suggestion that each European bird should be given a common and often even less interesting name. This is quite unnecessary when every bird in Europe and throughout the world already has an internationally accepted Latin name to assist the more serious birdwatcher.

There are two more Thrushes which visit us from North in winter, and these are the Fieldfare and its smaller cousin the Redwing, which can be seen throughout the South as far as Land's End when the weather further North is particularly severe and their food supply is either exhausted or covered in snow.

3

CORMORANTS AND SHAGS

Cormorants are often confused with Shags because they both appear black at a distance and look somewhat similar, but the Cormorant is larger and browner, with a white patch on the cheek and another on the thigh in the breeding season, whereas the Shag is smaller, greener, and sleeker, with a crest on its head when breeding.

The Cormorant's wing beat is slower than the Shag's, and the Cormorant, although basically a sea bird, is commonly seen in estuaries and on inland waters, even in the centre of London where it roosts in trees, whereas the Shag prefers salt water and rocky coasts. For this reason the Cormorant is commoner in the South East of Britain, with its absence of a rocky coastline, but elsewhere the two species overlap quite happily.

The young of both species are brownish with pale fronts, which can appear almost white in the case of immature Cormorants.

The Cormorant and the Shag have large webbed feet with

all four toes pointing forwards to provide quick propulsion under water when diving from the surface to chase fast swimming fish. They can dive quite deep and stay under water for considerable lengths of time, and to reduce buoyancy their feathers contain relatively little oil which is why they swim so low in the water and have to hang out their wings to dry after finishing a fishing foray. Both species lack the oil glands above the base of the tail which other birds use for preening feathers.

Another sea bird with large webbed feet and four toes pointing forward is the Gannet which dives on fish from the air and has to accelerate quickly to catch its prey, before rising to the surface to swallow its meal and get airborne again. Being a shallower diver, the Gannet's feathers are heavily oiled and it merely has to shake the water from its body as it leaves the water. One disadvantage of having heavily oiled feathers is that the oil is usually washed away when the bird has to be cleaned after being contaminated by an oil slick out at sea, and it is then sometimes necessary for the bird to be kept in captivity until it has moulted and grown new feathers, otherwise it would sink if released too soon back into the wild.

The nostrils of the Gannet, Cormorant and Shag are blocked to prevent the entry of water when diving deep or hitting the water at speed and they therefore have to breathe through open beaks. It is interesting to watch the contortions of fish and eels in the throats of Cormorants and Shags as the birds gulp down the poor protesting creatures. On the other hand, Herons, which fish from land, can usually bash fish senseless before swallowing them, but eels can still put up a stiff resistance by wrapping their bodies around the Heron's throat which covers their feathers in slime. However, the Heron has curious downy patches, or powder-puffs, on its breast and rump from which it collects powder-down on its head or beak to spread over any slime, which it then scrapes away with a pectinated or serrated middle toe, in the same way as we use a comb.

Another interesting thing about the large Heron is that it is mostly all beak, neck, feet and feathers, because its actual body is not much bigger than that of a small chicken.

Tragically for the Heron, and for the beautiful little Kingfisher, they both perish in large numbers in severe winters when shallows become covered in ice. Whereas Cormorants, Shags and the divers can always feed in deeper waters or out at sea.

4

CROWS AND ROOKS

The Crow family is very intelligent and consists of the glossy bluish-black Raven, which is the largest member with its huge black beak and wedge-shaped tail, and the usually solitary pairs of Carrion Crows, with the grey and black Hooded Crow, or Hoodie, taking their place in the North and in parts of Ireland, and then there is the gregarious Rook which lives in flocks and nests in rookeries. The Magpie and the beautiful Jay are also members of the Crow family, but they tend to be unpopular because they are not above taking the eggs and young of smaller birds in people's gardens.

Magpies have always been fairly common in villages and cities in many West European countries, particularly in those where people shoot, trap, snare and even pickle anything that moves in the countryside, but they have only recently moved into built-up areas in this country, where they are now so common that they can be seen nesting in the centre of London in Hyde Park and Kensington Gardens and even in the garden of Buckingham Palace.

Our remaining members of the Crow family are the cheeky, smaller Jackdaw, with their greyish napes and pale-grey eyes, which have become increasingly common in places like Cornwall, and lastly the rare aerobatic Chough, with its curved red bill and red legs, which is now extinct in Cornwall, where it is the County's National Bird, but can still be found in parts of Wales, Ireland and Scotland.

Some people tend to confuse the Carrion Crow with the Rook, but the Crow has a greenish-blue gloss to its plumage and dark feathers at the base of its beak and featherless legs, whereas the Rook's plumage has a purplish gloss and the base of its beak is bare and greyish and the top of its legs have feathered trousers. Also the Crow is solitary and is usually seen only in pairs, whereas the Rook is highly gregarious. It used to be said that if you see less than three Rooks they are Crows, and if there are more than two Crows they are Rooks, although you will obviously see small family parties of Crows during the breeding season, but, as so frequently happens with birds, there are exceptions to almost every rule, and I have seen over a hundred Carrion Crows feeding happily together in London's Kensington Gardens in early winter.

Ravens, Crows and Rooks are early nesters, with Ravens doing this presumably to take advantage of all the entrails available on which to feed their young at lambing time, and unless Crows and Rooks build their nests early they would have difficulty in getting large twigs and branches to the nest site once trees have become covered in leaves.

21

5

DIVERS AND GREBES

We have four different species of Divers in Britain. There is the Great Northern, the Red-throated and Black-throated, and the rarer White-billed. All are birds of the northern hemisphere, which are normally only seen in southern Britain in winter when there is severe cold weather further north.

Divers are the most primitive birds we have in this country, which means they are the closest to reptiles, which are the common ancestors of all birds, mammals and even man, and, as far as birds are concerned, the first known example of this ancestry was the Archaeopteryx which had some of the characteristics of both birds and reptiles.

Primitive birds have little or no song and build the simplest of nests, but many of them have the most fascinating and complicated courtship displays. Even if the Great Northern Diver cannot sing it has the most eerie and haunting call which has earned it the name of Loon in the North Americas.

The most primitive bird in the world is said to be the

Ostrich which, true to form, has no song and only a scrape in the sand for a nest and the most spectacular courtship display. It has lost the ability to fly because its size and fleetness of foot over the ground are sufficient to cope with any predator except for man with a gun.

Grebes are closely related to Divers and are almost as primitive. We have five different species which consist of the commonest, the Great Crested, and the fairly common Little Grebe or Dabchick, and the less common Black-necked and Red-necked, and the rarer Slavonian Grebe.

The Great Crested Grebe was in danger of becoming extinct at the turn of the last century because it was being shot for sport and for feathers to adorn the enormous women's hats which were fashionable in those days.

Luckily for this lovely bird, three intrepid ladies in northern England became so incensed at this slaughter that they formed a society to fight the feather trade, which was the forerunner of today's influential Royal Society for the Protection of Birds which now protects not only Grebes but all birds as well as their all-important habitat.

Although Grebes feed almost entirely under water, up-ending to dive down for considerable lengths of time, they do not have webbed feet like most water birds but only lobed toes like our ubiquitous Coot.

Grebes sit high on the water, looking something like large powder-puffs, because as soon as they surface they open out their feathers and close them again to trap a layer of air round their bodies to give them added buoyancy. Before submerging they compress their feathers to expel the air and become beautifully streamlined for their underwater existence. Sometimes, if a Grebe is alarmed, it will release this air and sink slowly under water until only its head is showing above the surface, like a submarine with a raised periscope, and it will remain there motionless until it sees

23

the coast is clear. Little Grebes, in particular, often use this form of defence as well as the commoner method of diving down to surface a long way away out of danger.

6

DUCKS AND GEESE

Our common wild duck is the Mallard which is the ancestor of all our domestic ducks, with the exception of the Muscovy which comes from the Latin Americas and not from Moscow, as the name might suggest.

Such diverse looking domestic ducks as the Khaki Campbell, the Indian Runner, the White Aylesbury and Call Ducks, and the common farmyard duck, have all been selectively bred from the Wild Mallard, and this is why all the males still possess the curled tail feathers of the Mallard drake.

The Mallard drake is more brightly coloured than the female which is well camouflaged to help it remain unnoticed on a nest. This difference in colouration occurs in most of the smaller members of the duck family, but the sexes look similar in the larger species, such as the Muscovy and the Shelduck, which presumably are big enough to defend themselves against most predators. The fact that the wild Muscovy nests in holes in trees and the Shelduck in burrows might be a reason why their females have no need for camouflage, but the smaller Mandarin and Carolina Ducks also nest in holes in trees and the females are much duller and better camouflaged than their colourful drakes.

When it comes to the largest members of the duck family, the Geese and the Swans, the sexes are similar and their size enables them to nest happily in the open on the ground without any need for cover or special camouflage.

Brightly coloured male birds don't need to be good songsters because they can rely on their colouring and display to attract a mate, and they leave the incubation of eggs to their less conspicuous females. Even the duck's loud quack comes from the female and not from the drake which only mutters away in a low-pitched key. Famous songsters like the Nightingale are not brightly coloured but inconspicuous, and so are Canaries in the wild. Captive Canaries are only bright yellow as the result of selective breeding which has also concentrated on developing the wild bird's natural ability to sing.

Most of our farmyard Geese are descended from the wild Greylag Goose of Europe which visits us in winter, but there is also the domestic Chinese Goose, with a dark line running down the back of the neck, which is descended from the wild Swan Goose of Eastern Russia and Northern Asia.

There are several alien species of Goose to be seen in parks and private collections, and some of these have escaped and a few now live here in the wild. The most successful of these is the Canada Goose which now lives and breeds happily throughout large areas of Britain. This is the famous migratory Goose of the North Americas which nests in northern Canada and spends the winter in huge flocks further south, as far as the Mexican border, to escape the northern snow and ice. In this country they might move to pair off in summer and to form flocks in winter, but they have no need to migrate because there is always food available wherever they happen to be. This supports the view that it is the search for food which dictates a bird's instinct to migrate, and not the climate, because they can withstand extremes of cold and heat provided they are able to feed.

Sea Ducks are more or less forced to submerge to feed, but only a few freshwater Ducks are true divers, like the Pochards and Sawbills, while others up-end and dabble at different depths like Swans, Mallard and Teal, and some feed chiefly on the shore or on land like Wigeon and Geese, whereas others, like the Shoveller, are quite happy to sift away for food on the surface or in shallow muddy water.

Most diving Ducks and all Geese and Swans have to patter along the surface when taking off from water, but some dabbling Ducks, like Mallard and Teal, can virtually explode into the air on take off, and climb away almost vertically when necessary, which is why they are able to frequent small pools even when they are surrounded by tall trees and buildings.

Young ducklings, goslings and cygnets are what is known as precocial or nidifugous, which means they are able to leave the nest and fend for themselves shortly after hatching. There are other such birds, like Pheasants, Partridges, Waders and farmyard chicks, but most birds are nidicolous and have to be fed by their parents until they have grown feathers and are able to fly; which can vary from about two weeks for smaller birds to three months for a Golden Eagle.

7

GULLS

We have five resident Gulls in Britain, consisting of the Black-headed, which happens to have a dark brown head in summer and a white one in winter, and the Common which is not that common, and the Herring which might have difficulty in finding a herring these days, and then there are the Great and Lesser Black-backed Gulls, with the Great having pink legs and the Lesser yellow ones.

Also, to add to the interest for birdwatchers, there is the Kittiwake, which only visits us in summer to breed because it is a true sea-gull, usually to be found far from shore, and the Glaucous and Iceland Gulls which often come here in winter to escape the freezing cold further north. Also various Mediterranean and North American Gulls appear from time to time, having lost their way or been blown off course during migration.

It is strange that in city parks, such as those in London, it is usually the Black-headed Gulls which scream to be fed, and will even take food from the hand, whereas where I come from in Cornwall it is the Herring Gulls which pester humans for food while any Black-headed Gulls in the vicinity appear unconcerned.

It is also strange that Gulls never think of placing a foot on what they are trying to eat, like so many other birds have learnt to do, when they are trying to peck out a tasty morsel from a dead fish or a bit of offal on the seashore. On the other hand some Gulls are clever enough to know they can persuade worms to come to the surface by pit-a-pattering on the ground with their feet, presumably to fool the creature into believing it is raining. However, this action is probably due more to instinct than to intelligence because they also do this on the concrete floors of the Mousehole Bird Hospital in Cornwall, and continue to do it throughout their stay even though nothing ever surfaces or is likely to do so.

This famous Bird Hospital was founded in 1928 by the late Yglesias sisters and is now run by a dedicated team of ladies named Olga, Jeanette, Janet, Amanda and Linda, with lots of local support, and with Jane and Kerry due to join the team while Jeanette looks after her new baby, Sam, and after Janet leaves to help her husband at his dental laboratory in Newlyn – the Bird Hospital relies on the public and legacies for financial help and is well worth a visit from anyone spending a holiday in West Cornwall.

8

JIZZ

Jizz is a useful word with which to impress a companion new to bird-watching. If asked how you were able to identify a bird which flashed past in a split second or appeared for a moment in a bush in the half-light, it sounds impressive to be able to say loftily that it was "by its Jizz, of course."

The word Jizz is believed to have been first used by the famous Cheshire Ornithologist, T.A. Coward, whose classic three volumes on *Birds of the British Isles* is a must for any birdwatcher's library.

Jizz covers absolutely everything about a bird and its habitat, including the time of year, day or night it is seen, and the weather locally and elsewhere at the time, and even the state of the tides.

Jizz also includes the size, shape, colouring and behaviour of the bird and how it flies and where it nests and on what it feeds.

Some birds soar, a few can hover, some flap slowly and others quickly, some whirr like the tiny Wren, and some alternately flap and glide. Other variations include the wing-beat of the Cuckoo which is downwards below the body, and a Pigeon's glide with wings held almost erect above the body. Also, a Cormorant's wing-beat is slower than a Shag's, and a Swift's wings appear to beat alternately compared with Swallows and Martins, and Woodpeckers, Little Owls and Mistle Thrushes which have a distinctly undulating flight. Most birds in flight appear to know exactly what they are doing and where they want to go, but charms or flocks of twittering Gold Finches and Linnets tend to jink this way and that, as if quite unconcerned where they are to, as the Cornish say.

One is unlikely to see a summer visitor in the middle of winter, although a few Chiffchaffs and Blackcaps now over-winter here in increasing numbers, or see winter visitors in the height of summer. One is just as unlikely to see oceanic birds inland, unless there are severe storms out at sea, or land birds over the ocean except on migration.

Some birds hop, some birds walk and others run, and some can both hop and walk, like Starlings and Crows, and others can walk and run like Wagtails and many Waders.

With all this Jizz rushing through the mind, an experienced birdwatcher can usually identify most birds in a flash, but one must always remember that there are freaks and exceptions, and also that bright sunlight or poor half-light can play strange tricks with a bird's shape and colouring.

It is lucky for birdwatchers and for Jizz that each species of bird produces offspring which are true to form, because just imagine the problems with identification if birds were like humans, with all our different coloured hair and eyes, and various shapes and sizes of heads, bodies, arms and legs.

One bird which varies almost as much as the Human Race is the male Ruff in the breeding season, when it develops display plumes around the head and nape which can be black

31

or white or various shades of speckled or striped greys or browns. However, when the female Reeve visits the display ground, or Lek, where the males are busy fighting and showing off their various ruffs, she appears to know which colour denotes virility because she invariably selects a Ruff with the darkest plumage, so perhaps Latins don't make lousy lovers after all.

9

KESTRELS

Like the Magpie, the Kestrel has become common in our inner cities, where it nests in church towers and steeples and on ledges in high buildings. In the countryside its main food consists of small mammals and large insects, which it also finds in abundance on the verges of motorways, but, as it is diurnal, and mice, shrews and large insects are rarely to be found on our city streets during daylight, the Kestrel has adopted a city diet consisting chiefly of smaller birds.

The verges along motorways are providing wonderful Nature Reserves, because they are relatively free from human and other disturbance, and another valuable haven for nature are the miles and miles of railway embankments, now that sparks from steam locomotives no longer set fire to the undergrowth. Just think what it would also mean for nature if the 2,000 or so Golf Clubs in Britain could be persuaded to give Natural History even the smallest consideration when managing the 'rough' and woodland on their courses, which could have the added benefit of saving the Club money on unnecessary upkeep.

Kestrels appear to be able to hover, but very few birds can actually do this in the true sense because it involves remaining stationary with rapid wing beats, holding the body at an angle of 45°, which is enormously energy consuming. Humming-birds can hover because they feed on nectar which provides plenty of energy, and so can Kingfishers for short periods before diving on a fish and emerging to swallow it whole, which also quickly replaces any loss of energy. The fish is always swallowed head first, so if you see a Kingfisher with a fish tail first in its beak, it is likely to be about to offer the catch to its mate, as part of its courtship display, or to its young in a nearby nest in a hole, in the bank on the water's edge.

What a Kestrel actually does when appearing to hover is to fly into the wind at the speed of the wind and thus remain stationary. Its old name was Windhover, so the early ornithologists at least got it half right. This is why Kestrels can be seen so-called hovering high up in the sky when there is little or no wind lower down, and almost at ground level when the wind is whistling over a cliff top.

The bastard wing, or alula, which are the feathers attached to the thumb in front of the wing, are particularly prominent on a Kestrel's wings which they use to reduce their stalling speed.

The Kestrel, like the Peregrine, is a true falcon, with its longish tail and narrow, pointed wings and rapid wing-beats, compared with the broader, rounded wings and slower wing-beats of the hawks, buzzards and eagles.

A Kestrel is the emblem of the Young Ornithologists' Club, or YOC, which is the youth section of the Royal Society for the Protection of Birds, with its own attractive coloured magazine, and a membership subscription makes a rewarding

34

present for anyone between the ages of about seven to
fourteen.

10

NESTING

Even the most talented architects like Wren, Adam and Lutyens had to spend years learning the secrets of their trade before they could put their skills into practice, but birds have to construct their nests, which are sometimes complicated and often beautiful, without the benefit of any advice or training.

A bird doesn't see its parents building the nest in which it was reared, and when it reaches adulthood it is unlikely to have seen another member of its species building one until it has to make one of its own, and yet it can construct an exact replica — which is something like asking an eighteen-year-old to design and build Saint Paul's Cathedral from scratch.

The world's most primitive bird is the Ostrich which merely lays eggs in a scrape in the sand, with several different females adding their eggs to the clutch and with the male undertaking the major share of the incubation. Further up the evolutionary scale, the primitive Divers and Grebes construct only rudimentary nests in the open, on or near a bank, but they have the intelligence to cover their eggs with whatever material is

36

available when they leave the nest in search of food.

But the more advanced birds can build very complicated nests which are sometimes lined with mud or feathers, and sometimes domed, and often beautifully decorated and camouflaged with lichen and moss like those of the Chaffinch, the Goldfinch, and the Long-tailed Tit.

Two of the most beautiful nests in Britain are the tiny ones made by Goldcrests, which they suspend beneath the branches of conifers with the help of gossamer from spiders' webs, and the domed, oval nest of the Long-tailed Tit, with an opening on the side near the top, which it fills with over 2000 tiny feathers. When the female Long-tailed Tit starts to lay she fits snugly in her nest, usually with her long tail sticking out through the opening, but as more eggs are layed and the young are hatched, sometimes up to a dozen or more, the feathered lining of the nest becomes compressed to enlarge the interior to whatever size the birds require.

The variety and methods of nesting are so numerous it is impossible to mention them all, but it would be interesting to know why Song Thrushes' nests are lined with mud, when those of the Blackbird and other Thrushes are not, and why the Magpie has a domed nest, when other members of the Crow family do not, and how male Brush Turkeys in Australia learn to control underground incubation temperatures by adding or scratching away earth and rotting vegetation on the huge mounds they build in which the female lays her eggs before deserting them completely.

11

OWLS

We have five different species of Owl in this country. The commonest are the Tawny Owls, which like woodland but also live happily in towns and villages where their familiar hoots and tu'wit tu'woos can often be heard at night, even in the centre of large cities like London. It is usually the male Tawny which produces the drawn out hoots and tu'woos, and the female which replies with the short sharp tu'wit. Then there is the ghostly Barn or Screech Owl, which is becoming increasingly rare because of changes in farming methods and the use of pesticides as well as the disappearance of old fashioned barns in which it liked to nest. There are also the Short-eared Owls of marsh and grassland, and the Lond-eared of woodland, and the much smaller Little Owl which was introduced from North America towards the end of the last century and has now spread to most parts of England and Wales.

Owls and birds of prey have little to fear from other avian predators, so their eyes face forwards and they have no need

38

to look continuously behind them to watch out for danger, like the smaller birds and rodents on which they prey. If they want to look sideways or behind them they have to turn their heads, which an Owl can do through about 180°. If you see an Owl perched on a branch or a post, it can be fun to walk round it in a circle and watch it turn its head through what looks like 360°, but, after traversing about half the way, it would have flicked its head round the other way, faster than the eye can see, and thus appear to have kept you in sight through a full circle.

Although most owls are chiefly nocturnal they have excellent eyesight by day as well as at night, and they have even better hearing, helped by their reflector-like facial discs and special wing feathers which enable them to fly without making a sound.

They use their hearing ability to detect the slightest movement or rustle while quartering the ground with noiseless flight or when perched somewhere, even on the darkest of nights.

Owls can reverse their outer toe if they so wish, with two toes forward and two backwards, to perch or grip their prey more firmly, and, like all birds of prey, they have large, sharp, pointed talons as opposed to a bird's normal nails or claws.

The so-called ear tufts on some owls are not connected with their true ears which are behind and slightly below the level of their eyes. These tufts can be raised to stand erect when the owl is nervous or inquisitive, but a bird's ears are usually hidden by smaller feathers known as ear coverts, although ears can be clearly seen on the naked heads of birds like Ostriches, Vultures, Turkeys and many domestic fowl.

Owl's eggs are round and white because they are usually laid in a covered hollow and cannot roll out and have no need for camouflage, compared, for instance, with those of Guillemots which are laid on narrow, open ledges and therefore have to be heavily marked and also conical in shape to prevent them falling over the side.

Owls regurgitate pellets to dispose of the feathers, fur and bones of their prey which they cannot digest properly. These pellets can help disclose an owl's nesting site or favourite roosting perch and they can also give a clue to the bird's predominant diet in any area. Other birds of prey produce these pellets, as do many smaller birds and some mammals like our native fox, and several sea birds like Cormorants and Shags do the same to dispose of fish bones and tough scales.

12

PIGEONS AND DOVES

The difference between Pigeons and Doves is that all Doves are Pigeons but not all Pigeons are Doves.

Our commonest Pigeon must surely be the London, Town or Feral Pigeon, descended from escaped domestic birds which have all been bred from the wild Rock Dove, no matter whether they are Racers, Pouters, Tumblers or even White Fantails.

Feral is the term used when a bird has escaped from captivity to establish itself successfully in the wild, and, apart from the Town Pigeon, other examples in Britain include the Canada Goose, the Pheasant, the Mandarin Duck, and the Ring-necked Parakeet.

The mixed domestic parentage of Town Pigeons accounts for the wide variations in their shapes and colours, but their offspring often eventually revert to resemble closely their ancestors, the Rock Doves, with blue-grey bodies and iridescent necks, two black wing-bars and prominent white rumps, and a black terminal band at the end of the tail.

c

Wild Rock Doves live in small flocks and nest in colonies on cliffs and in caves, and hence the Town Pigeon's preference for company and for ledges and buildings on which to roost and nest, whereas the larger Wood Pigeon still prefers trees, like its country cousins, even when living in city centres.

The Collared Dove is interesting because it was only first seen in England in the wild in 1952, having spread rapidly westwards across Europe from the Near and Middle East. When a pair first nested in East Anglia in 1954, it caused an ornithological sensation with excited birdwatchers coming from far and wide to have a look. Its numbers quickly increased to the extent that it is now almost a pest in some areas, and it has now spread further west to Ireland with North America as the only next stop. Some people believe that Collared Doves are partly responsible for the reduction in the number of the attractive Turtle Dove, which visits us in summer to breed, because they have taken over the Turtle Dove's habitat, but others think the decline could be due more to changes or persecution in the Turtle Dove's winter quarters in Africa.

Members of the Pigeon family can drink with their heads downwards, like humans and mammals, whereas other birds, including water birds, have to fill their beaks and throw their heads backward to have a drink. This is a priceless piece of useless information with which to impress your friends the next time you see a pigeon taking a sip from a puddle.

Pigeons have a very wide field of vision and can see through 340° without turning the head. However their binocular vision only extends 24° straight ahead, with monocular vision covering the other 316°, and the blind spot of 20° at the back of the head means it has to be turned constantly to keep watch directly behind.

Pigeons feed their young, or squabs, with regurgitated Pigeon's milk, which is a highly nutritious creamy liquid formed in their crops, which the squab obtains by inserting its beak down the throat of the parent. Wood Pigeons can raise as many as four broods of two young in a year, usually building a new nest for each brood, and they can sometimes be seen sitting on eggs in their new nest while still feeding young from the previous one.

13

ROBINS AND WRENS

The Robin and the Wren are two of our most attractive birds which are common in gardens. Both are highly territorial and the Robin will not even permit a member of the opposite sex into its territory outside the breeding season.

The busy little Wren is one of Europe's smallest birds, second only to the tiny Gold and Firecrests. For such a small bird the Wren has the loudest of songs which it belts out to attract a mate or proclaim a territory, which has to be relatively large due to its specialised diet of tiny insects, spiders and other minute creepy-crawlies.

At times the Wren has been considered the most numerous bird in Britain but it suffers terribly in the severest winters when its food either disappears or hides deep in cracks and crannies to escape the icy weather. Luckily, however, its numbers recover quickly due to the number of eggs it can lay and its ability to raise a large family.

The male is polygamous and usually builds up to four nests, but sometimes many more, which he shows to a mate who selects one and only then is it lined for her to lay her eggs.

The Robin is a relative of the Thrush family and the sexes in adults look identical, with their famous red breasts, but the brownish young have speckled breasts like the young of most other Thrushes.

When the Robin is ready to pair off he can be seen offering food tit-bits to invite his intended mate into his territory, but once nesting is over and the young have been fledged, he drives the mate and the offspring away to find territories of their own.

The Robin's song is loud and beautiful, and, with the Blackbird, it is the first to sing at dawn and the last to sing at night. It can often be heard at all hours of the night where there are street lights in towns and villages which appear to give it the impression of daylight. Its song can be heard in most months of the year, except during its moult after the breeding season when it likes to keep a low profile, and, if you are lucky, you might even hear a singing Robin on Christmas Day when everything is covered in snow.

The British Robin is a gardener's friend, feeding gratefully on insects and worms exposed by the digging of soil, and even perching on a spade's handle when the gardener takes a rest. It can easily be tempted to feed from the hand, particularly if luscious maggots are the food on offer. However, it is a different story in parts of Europe, where it is very wary of humans, especially in those countries where it knows it might end up in a pickling jar, where it is a shy woodland bird with duller plumage on its breast to make it less conspicuous.

14

SPARROWS

House Sparrows used to be one of the commonest birds in Britain and, although it is difficult to carry out an accurate census, especially in built up areas, there is little doubt that their numbers have recently declined for a variety of reasons.

The lack of horses and horse-drawn vehicles could have had some effect, because this has denied the sparrow one of its favourite sources of food scavenged from a horse's droppings. Being a seed eater, the poisons used on farmland must have also had an effect before these were banned and discontinued. Also the increasing numbers of Kestrels in towns and cities could be taking its toll because Sparrows form a major part of this Falcon's diet in urban areas.

Sparrows are a form of Weaver Bird which are believed to have come to Britain from the Mediterranean area during Roman times, following the Roman Legions and their horses across Europe, and hence their habit of living in small flocks and nesting in colonies with untidy weaver-type nests.

What used to be called a Hedgesparrow is now known as

a Dunnock because whereas the House Sparrow may not be a Sparrow the Dunnock is definitely not. It is an insect eater with a small thin bill and feeds mostly on the ground, moving furtively in little jerks like a mouse. The sexes are similar, with bluish-grey heads and breasts and dark brown streaks on the back and sides. It is a solitary bird with a weak but charming little song, usually delivered in spring and early summer from the top of a low bush or small tree.

The Dunnock was once listed as the most numerous bird in Britain until farming practices changed and hedgerows began to disappear, but this somewhat secretive bird is still very common even in central city parks and gardens.

A close relative of the House Sparrow is the less common and more rural Tree Sparrow which nests in holes in trees and cracks in walls. The sexes are similar and resemble the cock House Sparrow, although slightly smaller, more elegant, and with a chestnut crown instead of a grey one and a small black patch on each cheek.

15

STARLINGS

Starlings often earn themselves a bad reputation because they
are so aggressive and drive away smaller, more popular garden
birds to gobble up their food, but they are one of the most
interesting birds to study, and, if they were rare, they would
be considered quite beautiful, with their feathers reflecting
an iridescent sheen in the sunlight.

Starlings pair off in the breeding season to nest and rear
their young in holes in trees or in nooks and crannies in walls
and buildings, but in winter they forgather to roost at night in
flocks of hundreds of thousands. These huge roosting flocks
are often in trees and reed beds but sometimes on buildings
and under bridges in cities, including Central London.

A typical characteristic of Starlings is their distinctive
silhouette in flight, with their short tails and pointed wings,
which are wide at the base, and the way they fly. Before
descending from the sky to their winter roosts they fly in
their thousands this way and that, swirling in closely packed
formations without ever colliding, until they suddenly

decide to dive down crazily to alight on their chosen site.

Britain could never support these huge numbers of wintering birds if they all nested here and had to feed their young, so half the population leave these shores in early spring to breed in Northern Scandinavia and Russia, from whence they came to escape the deep snow and ice during the winter months. So there are British Starlings and Russian ones, just in the same way as there are British Swallows and South African ones, because some Swallows have to migrate North to breed while the others can remain in Africa permanently.

When Starlings are searching for food in soft ground, they appear to be jabbing their beaks into the earth with open mandibles, but they actually open them after each jab to search for food with their tongues. This must require the development of unusual muscles because creatures with even the strongest bites or grips, like dogs, crocodiles and lobsters, have difficulty in opening their mouths or claws if they are held closed with a human hand.

While foraging for food the Starling can swing its eyes forward and downwards to look along the beak and even between its open mandibles to spot a morsel to eat, and, without having to move its head, it can swing the eyes backwards and upwards again to watch out for danger from above and behind.

It is said that two elderly ladies in the last century imported into North America the fourteen garden birds mentioned in Shakespeare to establish them across the Atlantic. Of these, only the House Sparrow and the Starling have survived, to the extent that both are now considered pests and the House Sparrow can be seen as far South as Chile's Tierra del Fuego on the edge of Antarctica.

Shakespeare must have been quite an ornithologist because he mentions about sixty different species of birds in his works and describes them very well, whereas the Bible mentions only forty and gets many of them wrong, so one wonders what other biblical errors may exist.

The male Starling has a bluish base to its beak in the breeding season and the female has a pinkish one, so the sexes can be distinguished by remembering blue for a boy and pink for a girl.

16

STATISTICS

It is worth a reference to the Guinness Book of Records for interesting information about the world of nature, because everything is double checked before going to print, but the following items are a selection of facts about birds which might be of special interest.

The smallest bird in the world is the Bee Humming-bird of Cuba, and the biggest is the Ostrich of Africa, but the smallest and largest in Britain are the Gold and Firecrests and the Mute Swans.

The Bee Humming bird is only 5.9 millimetres or 2.25 inches long and weighs a mere 1.6 grammes or .055 ounces, so the bird could fit into a matchbox and two birds would weigh less than a single new penny piece. Our Goldcrests and Firecrests are approximately 9 millimetres or 3½ inches long and weigh about 4 grammes or .140 ounces, so they are half as long again as the Bee Humming-bird and weigh more than twice as much.

The Mute Swan is not only our largest bird but also the

world's second largest flying bird, losing first place only by a fraction to the Kori Bustard of East and South Africa, but their wing spans can nowhere near match those of the Wandering Albatross which measure up to 12 feet from wing tip to wing tip. Mute Swans are not completely mute and silent, and the description is believed to have originally referred to the low, muted sounds they sometimes make, compared to the loud honking or trumpeting of other Swans. They are, however, usually silent in flight except for the beautiful, haunting music created by their beating wings.

The bird with the widest vocabularly is possibly the Great Tit which is said to have as many as eighty different calls, although lacking any proper musical song. The sexes of Great Tits are easier to tell apart than with other members of the Tit family, because the male has a broad black band down its front which extends to between the legs, whereas the female's band is narrower and shorter.

The most numerous bird in the world is now thought to be the Red Billed Quelea which fly in huge flocks of over a million from the Sahara right down to South Africa, darkening the sky like a swarm of locusts before descending to cause havoc amongst the local crops. It was once thought that the Wilson's Storm Petrel was the world's most numerous bird, and although it is a bird of the open seas which is difficult to census accurately, it could still be among the most numerous since the sea covers two thirds of the Earth's surface.

Our own most numerous bird is almost certainly the Blackbird, with a population of fifteen to twenty million, but the Chaffinch, Dunnock and Wren have all vied for this honour in the past, until their numbers were reduced by farmland insecticides, the disappearance of hedgerows and some very severe winters. After the Blackbird, the next most numerous bird is probably still the Wren, which quickly recovers from disasters and now numbers about ten million or more, followed closely by the Robin with about ten million or slightly less. House Sparrows might reach somewhere near these numbers but they are extremely difficult to census, particularly in urban areas, and in any case the population appears to be on the decline in Britain.

It is difficult to name the rarest birds in the world because the situation keeps changing, with disappearing habitat having a disastrous effect on some species and with other endangered species beginning to enjoy a revival, thanks to help from man who is at last trying to do something positive about the protection of birds and their habitat. The captive breeding of endangered species for re-introduction back into the wild has also proved a success, like the Ne-Ne Geese bred at Slimbridge in Britain which are now thriving happily back on the volcanic slopes of Hawaii.

As the longest living birds have all been recorded in captivity they might have been unlikely to reach such ages in the wild, but it is interesting to know that a Cockatoo and a Condor have lived to an age of eighty, and a Siberian White Crane to the age of seventy. This suggests that in favourable circumstances some larger birds could share approximately the same life span as a human, but small birds are extremely lucky if they reach the age of three and luckier still to reach five, although some are able to reach about ten.

The highest flying bird to be recorded was a Whooper Swan which was seen by an aircraft pilot at over 27,000 feet or 8230 metres, but Swifts are also known to fly at very high altitudes. Pan Am airlines recently claimed that the nose of one of its Boeing 707s was dented by a goose flying at 33,000 feet which led to confirmation by Sir Peter Scott that Bar-headed geese were known to fly at this height over the Himalayas when migrating between India and Tibet.

53

The most aerial of birds is believed to be the Sooty Tern which remains out at sea for as long as three or four years, but our most aerial bird is the Swift which remains totally airborne from the time it is fledged from the nest until it is ready to breed in about two or three years time.

The fastest swimmer and deepest diver is the Penguin, which uses its wings to swim at considerable speed at great depths. Penguins are only found in the Antarctic and Polar Bears in the Arctic, although advertising agencies sometimes show them sharing the same ice floe when promoting mint sweets or frozen foods. An agency also once showed a golden packet of cigarettes nestling among sparkling jewellery in a Magpie's open nest whereas their nests happen to be domed.

The greatest distance travelled by any bird each year is probably by the Arctic Tern, which spends our summers in the Northern Hemisphere and our winters in the Antarctic, which enables it to enjoy almost permanent daylight, and in addition it is known to travel long distances across one ocean to another as well as from North to South and back again.

The most widespread bird in the world is the Barn Owl which can be found in almost every part of the world where it can find suitable food, although its numbers are unfortunately declining to an alarming extent in Britain.

The fastest flying birds in the world are believed to be some species of Duck and Geese although birds of prey like the Peregrine can reach considerable speeds at the end of a stoop, as can Swifts, in short bursts, during their courtship displays.

The slowest flying bird to progress forwards, as opposed to remaining stationary by hovering, is the American Woodcock which can fly at a speed at five miles per hour without stalling, so if a Cornishman tries to convince you that a Mevagissey Goose can fly backwards you should smile politely and offer him another drink, and, if you want to show off your knowledge, you could always add loftily you happen to know that only Humming-birds can fly backwards in still air.

The bird with the widest field of vision is the Woodcock which can see through 360° without turning the head, compared with a Pigeon's 340°. Woodcocks have monocular vision on each side but it is binocular straight ahead and slightly more so directly behind, because each eye can see through more than 180°, so they can literally see out of the back of their heads. This is why these beautifully camouflaged birds can sit tight on a nest, hidden among foliage on the ground, and remain motionless while watching your every move in any direction.

17

SWIFTS

Swifts are the most aerial of our birds which feed, drink, sleep, mate and collect nesting material on the wing and only descend from the sky to nest. The young, once they have left the nest, are completely independent and remain airborne until they are ready to breed in two or three years time, so they probably need a push from their parents to take off for the first time, knowing what future lies in store for them.

Swifts don't perch in trees or walk on the ground so their legs are small and weak, and their four toes face forward with strong little claws with which they can cling to perpendicular surfaces on landing, before crawling up like a bat to disappear into an eave or a belfry, or onto a ledge in a cave, where they like to build their cup-shaped nests.

Sometimes Swifts have to travel long distances to obtain sufficient insects to feed their brood, but the young can exist for relatively long periods without food by drawing on the fat in their bodies.

The Swift is one of the last summer migrants to arrive,

having flown all the way from south of the Equator in Africa, and one of the first to leave because they become torpid in cold weather. If there is a sudden cold spell they can sometimes be found on the ground, where, with their weak legs and long, scimitar shaped wings, they are unable to get airborne again. The answer is to pick them up gently and blow warm air on them before throwing them high into the air so they can fly safely away. Don't worry too much if you find large, ugly, long-legged ticks on their heads or bodies, because this is a common occurrence with Swifts and the ticks appear to do no permanent harm, but it would obviously be pleasanter for the bird if you could remove them.

Swifts are not related to Swallows and Martins, which look somewhat similar. Their nearest relatives are the Humming-birds of the New World which are more colourful and look quite different. This is a typical example of evolution where birds develop to suit their environment and feeding habits. Swifts, Swallows and Martins have evolved to look similar in appearance because their aerial life styles are similar, and Humming-birds have developed long bills, tubular tongues, and the ability to hover so they can extract nectar from flowers.

18

TREECREEPERS

Treecreepers are delightful little birds, which creep like mice up the trunks of trees and along branches, usually in a spiral fashion with frequent stops as they search for insects among the cracks in the bark. When they reach near the top of a tree they fly down to near the bottom of another one to continue their foraging upwards. They have stiff tail feathers, like a Woodpecker, which help to support them on their climb, and they never descend down the trunk of a tree, like a Nuthatch which is equally happy going up or down at will.

Treecreepers nest behind largish cracks in the bark and roost at night clinging closely to a tree's trunk. One of their favourite roosting places is against the trunks of Redwood trees, including the Giant Sequoia or Wellingtonia, which have been introduced from California and are now fairly common in parks and large gardens. These trees have a very soft, thick, fibrous reddish-brown bark which the Treecreeper can scrape away to form a shallow hollow to fit the shape of its body. If you see one of these scrapes with a trail of bird droppings on the bark underneath, it is worth approaching the tree quietly with a torch after dark in the hope of seeing the bird enjoying a quiet nap.

Our other birds which climb up trees are the large Green Woodpecker, or Yaffle, which is roughly the size of a Pigeon, the small Lesser Spotted Woodpecker which is not much bigger than a Sparrow, the Starling-sized Greater Spotted, and the small Wryneck, or Cuckoo's Mate, which is now a very rare summer visitor, looking nothing like a Woodpecker and lacking its stiff tail feathers. All four of these nest in holes, which both sexes of our three resident Woodpeckers can bore in trees with their strong, pointed beaks, and, when these holes are abandoned, there are plenty of birds like Tits, Pied Flycatchers, Starlings, Stock Doves and even the Wryneck, which are grateful for such ready-made nesting sites which they are unable to excavate for themselves. Where suitable trees are absent, as in parts of Cornwall, Green Woodpeckers have been known to nest in holes in old mine chimney stacks and even in holes in cliffs.

The only two Woodpeckers which can frequently be heard drumming in the breeding season are the Greater and Lesser Spotted, although the Green Woodpecker and Wryneck can also drum if they so wish. They do this to proclaim a territory and to attract a mate, with the Greater Spotted drumming faster, louder and longer than the Lesser Spotted.

It has nothing to do with feeding, which Woodpeckers and Nuthatches do by giving bark or dead wood a series of sharp taps to expose any grubs or insects which might be hiding inside. The Green Woodpecker and Wryneck are also very fond of ants, and they can often be seen feeding on the ground and even on lawns when ants are present.

Woodpeckers have sticky tongues, with backward facing horny barbs, which can be inserted deep into cracks and holes to extract insects and larvae.

19

WADERS

When one sees Waders in their thousands, and sometimes hundreds of thousands, all feeding together on mud-flats or along estuaries and the shoreline, it is difficult to imagine how there can be enough food to go round. The secret is that the mud or sand, on a receding tide, supports million upon million of worms, insects, crustaceans and shellfish of various shapes and sizes at different depths, and each species of bird, with its different length and shape of bill, can find all the food it needs without denying food to the others.

The Curlews and Whimbrels, with their long curved bills, and the Godwits, with their long straighter ones, can prod deep down for lug and rag worms. Then come the Shanks with their straight, shorter bills, and the Oystercatchers which can use their tough bills to chisel open mussels and cockles. Among the smaller Waders are the Turnstones, which upturn pebbles and seaweed to get at the food underneath, followed by the Sandpipers, Plovers, Knots, Dunlin,

d

Sanderlings and tiny Stints, which all manage to get their fair share on the surface or just below.

An interesting thing about Waders is that when they are suddenly disturbed by a Peregrine, a dog or a human, they can all get airborne simultaneously and wheel this way and that all over the sky in mass formations without a single collision. This is only possible because when they turn to the left, it is the birds on the extreme left which turn first and all others follow in a flash, just like aircraft in close formation, but much quicker, and if they change direction to the right, the first to turn would be the birds on the extreme right. In other words, the birds on each flank must always turn outwards, either to the left or to the right, followed by the others, otherwise there would be the most horrendous collision as any fighter pilot could tell you.

Sometimes, when an airborne flock is suddenly disturbed by a gun-shot, or a stooping Peregrine, it will split in two with half turning one way and half the other, but no collisions occur because the birds always obey the golden rules, and it is wonderful to see how the two halves join up again later without a single bird touching another.

It is also interesting how a Wader's daily life cycle is not controlled by the sun or by day and night, but by the moon and the tides. They feed on receding and incoming tides and roost and catch up on their sleep at high tide. If you can discover where Waders rest up at these times, usually somewhere near their feeding grounds but sometimes further inland, they can be ideal places for watching the birds as they preen or nap between courses so to speak.

Even when resting far inland, without being able to see or hear the sea, they somehow know when they must stir and head back to their feeding grounds, even during the hours of darkness and in spite of the tide times changing twice every twenty-four hours. This is the kind of mystery, like so many others in the world of birds, which makes bird-watching such an intriguing hobby.

20

WAGTAILS

Wagtails are so called because they constantly move their tails up and down, although they never actually wag them from side to side. They probably do this to help them blend in better with rippling water, since they are basically waterside birds, and it is thought that the Dipper, or Water Ousel, bobs up and down for the same reason when it perches on a rock or stone in a rushing stream. However, only the birds themselves and their Creator probably know for sure what they are to, as the Cornish say, because we humans can only speculate when it comes to understanding the reasoning behind some bird behaviour.

The Dipper is somewhat unique in that it can walk along the bed of a stream by gripping onto stones with its feet while searching for the larvae of aquatic insects and other titbits, but normally it prefers to swim along the bottom, using its wings instead of feet for propulsion, like a Penguin.

Our commonest Wagtail is the Pied Wagtail, or Water Wagtail as it used to be called, with its familiar black and white colouring and long tail which is held horizontally out of the way of wet and mud as it feeds along the water's edge. Its European sub-species, the White Wagtail, is paler and can often be seen in South Britain to test a birdwatcher's powers of identification.

Pied Wagtails sometimes forgather in large flocks at dusk in winter to roost communally in trees, reed beds or buildings where they huddle closely together for company and warmth, twittering away until they are ready to settle down for the night, when the twittering suddenly stops. By dawn the roosts have emptied, with nothing more than little messes underneath as the only evidence of their existence over night.

These roosts are sometimes suddenly abandoned for some reason or other and often occur in the centre of large cities like London and Dublin. There used to be a roost in London's Buckingham Palace Road, near Victoria Station, and there still may be the famous one in a tree in the middle of Hammersmith Broadway, near the tunnel entrance to the Underground which emits a stream of warm air up into the branches. The amber street lighting sometimes makes these Wagtails look yellowish which once led a distraught lady to telephone me in the middle of the night to report a thousand escaped Canaries in a tree and to ask what I proposed to do about it. An equally distraught lady once startled an RSPB Warden when she reported seeing a poor Puffin on the rocks with a carrot stuck in its mouth, which happily turned out to be a perfectly healthy Oystercatcher with a long orange beak.

Other Wagtails are the Yellow Wagtails, which are summer visitors, and the Grey Wagtails, which are an even brighter yellow and look very elegant with their extremely long tails. The Grey Wagtails like to spend the summer near mountain streams but in winter they come down to frequent sewage farms and the waterside around lakes and along rivers and the coast, and they can often be seen near water even in towns.

Closely related to Wagtails are the Pipits, and it is in the nests of the Meadow Pipit, together with those of the Dunnock and Reed Warblers, where Cuckoos like to lay their eggs. It was often thought that a Cuckoo could inspect the eggs in any nest and somehow produce an egg to match, after first throwing one out so that the number in the clutch remained the same. However, what usually happens is that Cuckoos choose to lay in a nest belonging to the same species as their foster-parents, as their own parents, grandparents and forbears are thought to have done, because their eggs happened to be a reasonable match, but how a Cuckoo knows this is a complete mystery, just as it is a mystery how a fully fledged young Cuckoo can find its way to Africa to join the adults which had long since left our shores, particulary when some of the resident foster-parents may never have travelled further than the next hedgerow or meadow.

21

THE FULMAR

My favourite sea bird is the Fulmar which I find fascinating for special reasons. It is not a gull, although of somewhat similar appearance, but a bird of the open seas, related to the Shearwaters and Petrels. Like them, it has a tubular nose which is designed to help it dispose of surplus salt from the sea water scooped up when feeding on the surface of the ocean. Also, like them, it only comes on land to breed, which it does in small colonies on rocks and cliffs along our coasts, and when it lands on a suitable ledge it can only shuffle along on bended feet because it has lost the ability to walk normally after spending so much time at sea. These nesting colonies used to be fairly rare but their numbers have increased considerably recently and some can now even be found on ruined buildings several miles inland.

It is said that when R.J. Mitchell was designing his famous Spitfire he used to lie on his back on a cliff top and watch the flight of gulls to give him inspiration. However, the Spitfire's Chief Test Pilot, Jeffery Quill, tells me that this would have been most unlikely with such a professional at such an advanced stage of aircraft design, even though Leslie Howard, who played Mitchell in the film *The First of the Few*, was shown watching gulls in this way to help perpetuate the legend. In any event, even if this story is only half true, Mitchell could never have got his inspiration from any gull but he could have got it from a Fulmar, which flies with a more rapid wing beat and loves to glide down and soar up the face of rocks and cliffs, with stiff, elliptical, pointed wings, just like a Spitfire's, before executing a stall turn at the top to dive down at speed for the next soaring climb. Fulmars even have what look something like RAF markings on the top of each wing near the tip.

Fulmars protect their nests by spitting a foul smelling oil over anybody or anything they consider a danger, including unfortunate rock climbers who chance to come too close, in the same way as the Spitfire spat deadly lead at its enemies. Young Fulmars can also defend themselves in the same way, and even their own parents have to approach with caution.

As an old Spitfire pilot myself, I love to watch the Fulmars which now breed all along the coast between Mousehole, where I live, and Lamorna in beautiful Cornwall, and I like to imagine that each of them represents one of the wartime Spitfires which ended up so tragically at the bottom of the sea further out in the English Channel.

68

INDEX